MYTH MEN

GUARDIANS OF THE LEGEND

HERCULES

THE STRONG MAN

BY LAURA GERINGER

ILLUSTRATED BY PETER BOLLINGER

SCHOLASTIC INC.

NEW YORK TORONTO LONDON AUCKLAND SYDNEY

For Ethan, my own superhero. —L. G.   *For my family. —P. B.*

Text copyright © 1996 by Laura Geringer. • Illustrations copyright © 1996 by Peter Bollinger. MYTH MEN is a trademark of Laura Geringer and Peter Bollinger. • All rights reserved. Published by Scholastic Inc. • Book design by David Saylor.

12 11 10 9 8 7 6 5 4 3 2 1   6 7 8 9/9 0 1/0
Printed in the U.S.A.   08
First Scholastic printing, August 1996

1

ONCE THERE WAS a hero named Hercules. He was very strong and very brave. He had big muscles — the biggest in the world. From the day he was born, he went around the world having adventures. Some people say he was not very smart, but that's not true. And here is a story to prove it.

One day, Hercules went to work for a bad king. The king hated Hercules. He spent all of his time thinking up dangerous things for the hero to do.

First, he sent Hercules to fight the fierce Lion of Nemea. The lion was eating people all over Greece, but Hercules put an end to him!

Next, the king sent Hercules to a dark swamp to face the Hydra, a man-eating monster with nine heads. As soon as Hercules cut off one head, two more grew in its place. And the last would not stop biting — even after it was cut off!

Then the bad king ordered Hercules to wrestle Geryon, a cattle rancher with three ugly heads, six legs, six arms, and six heavy clubs in his six hands.

To make matters worse, Geryon had a nasty two-headed dog with very sharp teeth!

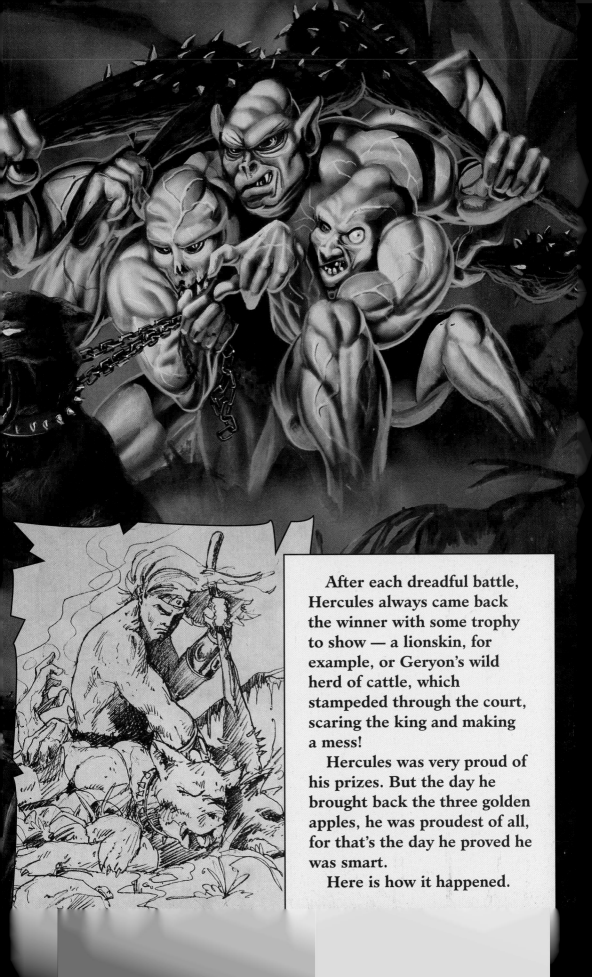

After each dreadful battle, Hercules always came back the winner with some trophy to show — a lionskin, for example, or Geryon's wild herd of cattle, which stampeded through the court, scaring the king and making a mess!

Hercules was very proud of his prizes. But the day he brought back the three golden apples, he was proudest of all, for that's the day he proved he was smart.

Here is how it happened.

THE GOLDEN APPLES grew on a golden tree in the magic garden of the Hesperides. And that golden tree was guarded by a terrible dragon. Now, Hercules was not afraid of the dragon. But he should have been, because it had one hundred heads!

On his way to fight the dragon, Hercules met three young nymphs who offered him advice.

"Go back, Hercules," they cried. "We do not want the dragon with one hundred heads to eat you up!"

Hercules laughed. "The Hydra didn't eat me up," he said. "Geryon and his two-headed dog didn't eat me up, either. I'm not afraid of the dragon with one hundred heads!"

So the nymphs pointed Hercules toward the sea. "Find the Old One," they said. "And when you find him, hold on tight. No matter what happens, DO NOT LET HIM GO!"

Hercules thanked the nymphs and traveled on until he came to a great cliff above a white sand beach. There he saw the Old One, sleeping in the surf below. With a mighty leap, Hercules sprang into the crashing waves. He landed on top of the strange old man, grabbing him firmly by the leg.

But was the Old One a man after all?

His feet were webbed. His long beard was seaweed green. And his body was covered with fish scales.

OLD ONE, WHICH WAY TO THE GARDEN OF THE GOLDEN APPLES?

In a flash, the Old One changed into a giant albatross! The wild seabird shrieked and struggled to break away, but Hercules held on tight.

All at once, the albatross was gone! It had changed into a huge serpent. Wrapping itself around the hero's neck, it opened its deadly jaws to devour him.

For the first time, Hercules felt afraid. He had nearly been strangled to death by just such a snake when he was a baby! But he was smart enough to know that the Old One was playing tricks on him. So Hercules squeezed and squeezed until the serpent's hiss was heard all the way around the world.

3

THE OLD ONE disappeared into the sea. Shading his eyes, Hercules looked toward the horizon. Something gleamed brightly like the sun. But, unlike the sun, it was coming straight toward him on the rising tide.

It was a giant cup!

Tired from his battle with the Old One, Hercules climbed into the cup, lay down, and let the waves rock him to sleep.

Hercules slept for a long time. Suddenly a loud noise startled him awake. The cup had crashed into a rock! Tossing wildly, it spun around and around, knocking into one rock after another and ringing like a bell. Finally, it swept ashore on an island.

Hercules grabbed on to a huge boulder and climbed out of the churning sea.

But when he looked closer, the boulder turned out to be the largest foot he had ever seen!

Oak trees grew between the toes. And as Hercules looked up and up . . .

. . . he found himself staring into the face of a giant. And such a giant!

He was as tall as the tallest mountain. Clouds rested around his middle. And most wonderful of all, he was holding up the sky!

But Atlas sounded tired. And Hercules, who had traveled far and wide, was smart enough to know that tired sound.

"My friend," he said, and the giant started with surprise, for no one had called him a friend in a thousand years.

MY FRIEND, YOU HAVE BEEN HOLDING UP THE SKY FOR A LONG TIME. IS IT *VERY HEAVY?*

NOT AT FIRST, BUT IT GETS HEAVY AFTER A *THOUSAND YEARS.*

Now, Hercules had been warned by the Old One, but it seemed to him that holding up the sky was a greater feat than slaying a dragon with one hundred heads. So he began to climb up, up, up . . .

     . . . until he reached the top of the nearest mountain. And from that height, he faced Atlas. They stood that way for a long while, taking one another's measure. Then Hercules nodded.

"I'LL DO IT!" he cried.

Slowly, Atlas shifted the weight of the sky to the hero's shoulders. And when this was done, Atlas stretched and lifted first one foot and then the other out of the forest that had grown around them. Then he gave a loud whoop, and began to leap and dance, flinging himself high into the air and coming down again with a shock that made the whole Earth tremble.

He stepped into the waves, ten miles at first stride, ten miles at the second, ten miles more at the third, until he stood in water to his waist, like a great god of the sea.

Then he turned, waved at Hercules, and dropped out of sight.

Hercules heard the Old One's words echoing in his head: "No matter what happens, DO NOT LET THAT GIANT TRICK YOU INTO HOLDING UP THE SKY!"

He thought of all the people in his life who were of the opinion that he wasn't too smart. And he thought they were right. But Atlas had promised he would be back before Hercules could say "golden apples of the Garden of the Hesperides" ten times. And a promise was a promise. So Hercules began....

4

HERCULES WISHED HE were a shepherd, or a farmer, or even a goat or a pig, instead of a hero holding up the sky. "Golden Apples of the Garden of the Hesperides . . ." he said for the nine hundred and twenty-fifth time.

"Hercules!" called a deep voice in the distance. "The dragon with one hundred heads is a sight to see. Too bad you missed him."

There, to his great relief, was Atlas striding toward him, juggling three golden apples as big as pumpkins in his hands.

ATLAS! COME QUICKLY AND TAKE THE SKY. I DON'T KNOW HOW MUCH LONGER I CAN HOLD IT!

The giant chucked the golden apples into the air twenty miles high and caught them as they came down. "You're a strong man, Hercules," he said, "and you've found no better way to prove it. The children of the future will say, 'He was so strong, he held up the sky!'"

Hercules kept on going, juggling the three golden apples as he went. And they gleamed high in the sky like three setting suns.

Atlas was right, of course. The children of the future did hear the story of Hercules and the golden apples over and over again. But when anyone who knew Hercules told it, they did not say, "And that, my children, is how Hercules proved he was strong enough to hold up the sky."

Oh, no. Instead they said, "And that, my children, is how Hercules proved he was smart."